Hollywood 101

24-CARAT COMMERCIALS for kids

"Everything Kids Need To Know To Break Into Commercials!"

by

Chambers Stevens

Sandcastle Publishing
South Pasadena, California

24-Carat Commercials for Kids! Everything Kids Need To Know To Break Into Commercials
Copyright © 1999 by Chambers Stevens
Book Cover & Interior Design by Renee Rolle-Whatley
Book Cover Photography by Karl Preston
The images used herein were obtained from IMSI's Master Clips©/MasterPhotos© Collection, 1895
Francisco Blvd. East, San Rafael, CA 94901-5506, USA

Actors in Cover Photograph: Left-to-Right: Back Row: Saroya Whatley, Scarlett Pomers, Michael Allen
Moreno Front Row: Andrew Harter
Storyboard Graphic by Jeremy Cohen

Published by: Sandcastle Publishing & Distribution

Post Office Box 3070
South Pasadena, CA 91031-6070
Phone/FAX (323) 255-3616.

Publisher's Cataloging in Publication

(Provided by Quality Books, Inc.)
Stevens, Chambers.
    24 Carat Commercials For Kids! : everything
kids need to know to break into commercials / by
Chambers Stevens. -- 1st ed.
    p. cm. -- (Hollywood 101 ; #2)
    Includes bibliographical references and index.
    LCCN: 98-75168
    ISBN: 1-883995-09-4
    SUMMARY: Explains now children and young people
can secure an agent and a work permit, prepare a résumé,
and learn to perform professionally in commercials.

    1. Acting for television--Vocational guidance--United States--Juvenile
literature. 2. Child actors--United States. 3. Television advertising--
Vocational guidance--United States--Juvenile literature. 4. Radio
advertising--Vocational guidance--United States--Juvenile literature.
I. Title

PN2055.S84 1999   791'.023'75
                              QBI99-529

Printed and bound in the United States of America
02 01 00 99   10 9 8 7 6 5 4 3 2

What Others Are Saying About 24-Carat Commercials for Kids

"Working with Chambers has taught me how to keep it honest, fun and real. That's how I continue to book commercials."

—CHUCK MONTGOMERY, ACTOR
COKE, BURGER KING, GENERAL MOTORS, US NAVY

"Since I've been working with Chambers, my commercial technique has improved 110%."

—LEANNA BOYER, ACTRESS, *MINUTE MAID, PEPSI, GUSHERS*

"Chambers puts the fun in acting! It takes a lot of fun to book 33 commercials."

—SCARLETT POMERS, ACTRESS
CAMBELLS SOUP, MCDONALDS, MATTELL TOYS, KRAFT CHEESE

"Before I started working with Chambers, my career was at a standstill. A couple of months later, I had a manager, an agent and the confidence to win the Miss City of Los Angeles pageant."

—VANESSA MENENDEZ, *MISS CITY OF LOS ANGELES*

"After working with Chambers for a couple of months, I booked my first audition! A 15-part commercial. I was on the set all summer!"

—CHAD MOSELEY, ACTOR

"Chambers' expertise will take you on a road trip through Hollywood. It's great to have a guide when you go there."

—BARRY COHEN, EDITOR, *NICKELODEON*

24-Carat Commercials for Kids!

What Others Are Saying About Chambers Stevens

"I can always count on Chambers Stevens to provide me with solid, experienced and talented child actors."

—EMILY DES HOTEL, CASTING DIRECTOR, *SUSAN VASH CASTING*

"I always see the genuine trust that kids have for Chambers. It allows them to be free in their craft."

—SCOTT DUNCAN, VP, *TRILLION PICTURES*

"What separates Chambers is his compelling skill as an actor/writer."

—JASON MCCLOSKEY, *DRAMA-LOGUE*

"Chambers is a versatile writer/actor of unusual potential. He is a theater professional of high energy and enthusiasm."

—CLARA HIERONYMUS THEATRE CRITIC, *THE TENNESSEAN*

"Chambers Stevens is magic. He has the uncanny ability to bring out the absolute best in every single child he coaches. I wish I were a child again so that I could have Chambers as a coach!"

—MAE ROSS, PRODUCER, *CHILDREN'S TALENT SHOWCASE*

"Chambers' success as an acting coach for kids is the result of the knack he has for finding the best in each child and drawing it out with his wonderful sense of fun and enthusiasm."

—TEMPLE LYMBERIS, DIR. OF LEARNING SERVICES, MISSISSIPPI ETV

"Chambers discovers what's funny in the trials and tribulations of growing up."

—BARBARA MULTER, PRODUCER, SHOWTIME

Everything Kids Need To Know To Break Into Commercials!

Table of Contents

Dedication

TO

AUSTIN CHAMBERS

WHO TAUGHT ME THAT
THE ONLY LIFE WORTH LIVING,
IS ONE CHASING YOUR DREAM.

$538 Million Dollars!

$538 million dollars! That is how much money American actors made doing commercials last year*. I'm sure you're not surprised. Everywhere you look there are commercials, commercials, commercials! You can't turn on the television, radio or even go to the movies without running into commercials.

For the last twelve years, I have been a kid's acting coach. Just like Michael Jordan—the world's greatest basketball player—had a coach, many actors do too. I have coached kids in shows for Nickelodeon, Disney, CBS, NBC, ABC and FOX plus countless movies and theater productions. I have helped kids get agents, managers, Broadway shows—even the lead in the school play! But the largest group of kids I've coached has worked in commercials. Many of them have done 20 or more. As an actor, I have been in 50 myself. Last year, I coached a young actress who had done over 100 commercials. And she was only eleven!

The book you are holding is what I've learned coaching over a thousand kids. It's everything you need to know to get started in commercials. I'll go over how to get an agent, pictures and even how to audition. Have fun with the commercials in the book. Practice them. Like everything in life, practice makes perfect. Who knows, the next time you turn on your television, you might just see yourself.

*The Hollywood Reporter- March 17, 1998

Introduction

 Question: If your dream is to play on a major league baseball team, what is the first thing you need to do to reach your goal?

A. Get a sports agent.

B. Tryout for a major league team like the St. Louis Cardinals or the LA Dodgers.

C. Go in the backyard and work on your batting and pitching.

The answer is obviously C. You will never be able to play for the NY Yankees unless you first can play baseball. It takes a lot of *practice* before you can play in the World Series.

Well, it's the same with being a commercial actor. Before you can get a commercial, you need to *practice* commercials. How, you say? Well aren't you lucky? This book has over 100 commercials to work on. So let's get to it.

Here's a typical commercial script:

OREOS

Everybody has their favorite way of eating Oreos. Some people eat the cookie first. Some people eat the middle. Me? I just pop the whole cookie in my mouth.

Announcer: Oreos. They taste good no matter how you eat them.

I'm sure you've seen millions of commercials just like this on television. Well, let me ask you a question. Of all the words in the oreo commercial, what do you think is the single most important word?

If you said "Oreos", you are right.

In fact, if you wanted to, you could rewrite the commercial just like this:

OREOS
Oreos Oreos.

Announcer - Oreos Oreos Oreos Oreos Oreos.

You see, the people making commercials care about only one thing: selling the product. So when you work on commercials, you have to remember the same thing. If you are not helping them sell the product, then you are not doing your job.

Rule #1 - Always remember that commercials are for selling the product.

Okay, now let's actually work on a commercial. Here's one about Mrs. Warner's Frozen Corn.

CORN

I used to hate vegetables. Until I discovered Mrs. Warner's frozen corn. Just put it in the microwave and a minute later you have a tasty treat. Mrs. Warner's Frozen Corn comes creamed or on the cob. Get yours at your grocer's freezer today.

What is the most important thing about this commercial? I hope you said, "Mrs. Warner's Frozen Corn". Selling Mrs. Warner's Frozen Corn is your main goal.

Now I want you to take a couple of minutes and memorize the commercial. When my students first come to me, it usually takes them 20 minutes to memorize a commercial. But after a couple of weeks, they can memorize one in 5 minutes. Just like everything, *practice* makes perfect.

The best way to memorize a commercial is to read it over and over and over again. Ten or fifteen times. And read it out loud. Hearing the commercial as you are saying it, really helps you memorize faster.

EXERCISE: MEMORIZE COMMERCIAL

Okay, have you got it memorized? If you haven't, DO NOT GO ANY FURTHER!

If you think you have it memorized, then I want you to do another exercise.

Stand up. Now do 15 jumping jacks.

EXERCISE: DO 15 JUMPING JACKS

Finished? Okay, now I want you to do 15 jumping jacks and say your commercial at the same time.

On your mark. Get set. Go.

EXERCISE: DO 15 JUMPING JACKS WHILE SAYING YOUR CORN COMMERCIAL

How did you do? If you didn't mess up at all, then you have it memorized. If you messed up—well, sorry, but you don't have it memorized.

You see, if you can do two things at the same time, then you have it memorized. When you audition for commercials, you *will* get nervous. Everyone does. Having your commercial memorized, and I mean really memorized, will help you not mess up.

Here is another great exercise to see if you have your commercial memorized. Get a deck of cards. As you say your commercial, you are going to make two piles: one with red cards and one with black. Make the piles very quickly. If you can do this without messing up the cards or the commercial, then you have it memorized.

OPTIONAL EXERCISE: DO COMMERCIAL WHILE SORTING CARDS

Rule #2 - Memorize your commercial. Test yourself to make sure it is really memorized.

Now back to our corn commercial.

Stand up. Pick a point on the wall. Make sure you are not standing too close to the point. This is going to be your camera, so you'll want to talk to the camera.

Run through your commercial one time. Remember when you say the words, "Mrs. Warner's Frozen Corn", smile a little. If *you* don't like the product, then you cannot sell it.

EXERCISE: DO EXERCISE LOOKING AT WALL

How did you do? Was it hard talking to the wall? A lot of kids find this difficult at first. But practice makes perfect. Almost all commercial auditions are on camera. So getting comfortable talking to the camera is very, very important. This is so important that I made it rule # 3.

Rule #3 - Get comfortable talking to the camera.

The best way to get comfortable is to pretend that the camera is your best friend. Who is your best friend?

Stand up. Look again at the point on the wall. Now pretend that your best friend is standing there. Using the words of the script, tell him/her how much you like Mrs. Warner's Frozen Corn.

EXERCISE: DO COMMERCIAL PRETENDING TO TALK TO YOUR BEST FRIEND

Wasn't that much easier? And I'll bet you were a lot more natural.

Okay, find a book. Not too big. Do you have it? We are going to pretend the book is your package of corn.

Now the only thing more important than how you *say* the product name, is how you *treat* the product on camera. Take a box of cereal, for example. It takes tens of thousands of dollars to design a cereal box. The design costs more than most diamonds. Do you understand why the cereal makers want you, the actor, to treat their product with respect?

Rule #4 - Treat the product with respect.

So hold the book toward the camera. Make sure your hands aren't covering the front. Now do your commercial again, but this time, use the book as a package of corn.

First Things First

EXERCISE: DO COMMERCIAL USING PROP

Was it hard? It will take some practice. As you're work-ing with props, make sure you hold them high enough. I've found that most young actors hold props near the waist instead of near the chest. Turn on the television and look how other actors are using props. See how they are treating the product with respect? With practice, you'll be doing that, too. So keep practicing.

Here are our 4 rules. Memorize them, too!

Rule # 1 - Always remember that com-mercials are for selling the product.

Rule # 2 - Memorize your commer-cial. Test yourself to make sure it is really memorized.

Rule # 3 - Get comfortable talking to the camera.

Rule # 4 - Treat the product with respect.

Before you start working on commercials, you should also always warm up your body and voice. Just like athletes and dancers warm up before they start their games or perfor-mances, actors also need to get their bodies and voices ready for work.

EXERCISE - WARMING UP YOUR BODY

1. Stand up. Pretend you are standing under an apple tree and there is an apple just out of reach. Really reach for it. Do you feel the stretch?
2. Do ten jumping jacks. Then run in place for ten seconds. Your heart should really be pumping now.

Equally important is warming up your mouth. Over the years I have found the best way to do this is by saying some *tongue twisters*. They are the perfect thing to get your mouth really working.

EXERCISE - WARMING UP YOUR MOUTH

Repeat each tongue twister 5 times fast:

1. A big black bug bit a big black bear and made the big black bear bleed blood
2. Through thick and thin
3. The red rat ran rapidly
4. The lips, the teeth, the tip of the tongue
5. Lovely Lucy loves Larry
6. Silly Sally sells seashells by the seashore
7. Peter Piper the pepper picker picked a peck of pickled peppers

Did you say each tongue twister 5 times? I'll bet you are warmed up now. Okay, time to work on commercials.

24-Carat

Commercials

for Kids

Commercials for Girls

Okay, girls, these commercials were written just for you. Practice with props (lipstick, brushes, etc.). You need to get comfortable using all types of props on camera.

1.　AMERICAN AIRLINES

Hey, Mom, you are probably wondering how I got on TV. It doesn't matter. I'll tell you about it later. The important thing is, I'm in Hawaii! Doesn't it look beautiful? See, there is the beach and the ocean and *(walking by a small shop)* tons of great places to shop. So, Mom, I know you need a vacation as much as I do. So hop on American Airlines and have them fly you to Hawaii. *(She walks by the shop again.)* Oh and bring your checkbook. I'm running out of money.

2.　LIPSTICK BY HELENA

The problem with lipstick is it never stays on for longer than five minutes. And it usually ends up on my teeth. No girl looks pretty with red teeth. But now I use Long Last by Helena. It stays on for hours and best of all, it leaves your teeth white. And it comes in forty different colors. Don't they look great?

3.　MAC BLUSH

Have you ever seen those women who wear too much blush? It looks like they have clown make-up on. What they need is a makeover by Mac. Every Mac store is staffed with the best makeup professionals. They'll help you find the look that's best for you. So if you look like you belong in the circus, go to Mac today.

4.   IMAC COMPUTER - GIRL

Dear Grandma. Thanks for sending me the iMac computer for Christmas. It sure beats the shirt you sent me last year. And the doll you sent me the year before. And the book you sent me two years ago. And the microwave you sent me the year before that. And the—

(Fade out as the announcer comes up)
Announcer - iMac. More than a computer.

5.   ST. IVES LOTION

I may be a kid, but my skin feels like I'm eighty years old. So Mom gave me St. Ives lotion. I put it on right after getting out of the shower. The coca butter makes my skin soft. And it smells like a sweet summer rain. So if your skin feels like your grandmother's, get your mom to get you St. Ives.

6.   JOHNSON'S NO MORE TANGLES

Tangles. Tangles. Tangles. When you have long hair like mine, tangles are your biggest enemy. But now I've got serious protection on my side. Johnson's No More Tangles. Just spray it on and tangles go bye-bye. Now, if I could just get rid of my dandruff.

7.   BUBBLEGUM TOOTHPASTE

If there is one thing I hate, it's the taste of toothpaste. Yuck! It's like putting chalk in your mouth. When my dentist heard about my problem, he gave me new bubblegum-flavored Best. It still cleans my teeth, but now it's bubblegum-flavored. Thank you Best!

8.   RAMPAGE

On the first day of school I want to be noticed. So I got Mom to
take me to Rampage. They have cool back-to-school clothes.
Jeans, tops and millions of cool earrings. You can bet on my first
day back to school, I'm going to be stylin'!

9.   LOVE'S BABY SOFT

So Jesse walks up to me in PE and says, "Wow you smell good".
Just like that! "Wow you smell good". So I said, "It's Love's Baby
Soft!" And then he says, "Let me see," and he hugs me right there
in PE. And then he goes, "Yep you feel pretty soft to me." I almost
fainted. Who knew smelling like a baby would help get guys?

10.   EXACT

It was the day before the homecoming dance and I had a huge zit on
my chin. So my best friend Jamie gave me Vanishing Cream by
Exact. It's patented formula went right to work and in a matter of
hours, my pimple was gone. So now I'm using Exact's Face Wash so
the zits stay away forever. I'm only a freshman. I've got a lot more
homecomings to go.

11.   SCHICK

One day at the pool some boys started making fun of me 'cause I
had hair on my legs. I told my mom. The next day she gave me a
Schick Silk Effects razor. The only razor with protective guard
wires that keeps you from cutting yourself. Now my legs look
smooth. Wait till those boys at the pool see them now.

Okay, guys, here are some commercials just for you. Remember to memorize them, word perfect. And practice using hand gestures. In my coaching, I've noticed that most young male actors just put their hands in their pockets instead of gesturing. And don't forget to smile. Remember, you are trying to *sell* the product.

13. VITAMINS

When I was a kid, I took vitamins that looked like superheros and cartoon characters. But they tasted like candy. Mom had to buy those kind, otherwise I wouldn't have eaten them. But now that I'm a teenager, I take Power Vitamins. They're not cute or sugar-coated, but they are powerful. *(Flexing his muscles)* Can't you tell?

14. AMERICAN AIRLINES

Hey, Dad, you are probably wondering how I got on TV. It doesn't matter. I'll tell you about it later. The important thing is I'm in Hawaii. Doesn't it look beautiful? See, there is the beach and the ocean and *(a pretty girl walks by)* well there are tons of beautiful sights here. So Dad, I know you need a vacation as much as I do. So hop on American Airlines and have them fly you to Hawaii. *(The girl walks by again)* You won't regret it.

15. CONVERSE

I used to be one of those kids who had to have the latest sports shoes. Michael Jordan's. Charles Barclay's. Shaq's. Then I discovered Converse. They come in tons of colors and never go out of style. Converse.

16.   WORLD WIDE WRESTLING

My dad said, "Give me one good reason we should get cable." I said, "Cable gives you 24-hour World Wide Wrestling." He said, "WWF is on 24 hours a day?" I said, "Yep." He said, "That's good enough for me." Aren't dads great?

17.   PLAYSTATION

Metal Gear Solid, Final Fantasy VIII, Mortal Kombat 4, Twisted Metal 2, Crash Bandicoot 2, Tomb Raider 3, NFL 99. Playstation. How many reasons do you need?

18.   BALL PARK FRANKS

My dad likes Ball Park Franks with mustard. I like Ball Park Franks with mustard. My dad eats his Ball Park Frank with one hand. I eat my Ball Park Frank with one hand. My dad says Ball Park Franks are the best hot dog in the world. I say—well you get the idea.

19.   CLEARASIL

When I get a zit and I want to zap it, I use Clearasil. It's tough like me. Clearasil. The zit zapper.

20.   FENDER GUITARS

When my parents asked me what I wanted for Christmas I said, "A Fender Guitar!" My dad was like, "Why a Fender?" *(Jams on his air guitar making heavy metal sounds)* That's why!

21. Gillette Ultra

I wake up this morning and walk into the bathroom. And there on the sink is a brand new Gillette Ultra razor and a can of shaving cream. Somebody was trying to send me a message. So I wet my face. Put a little shaving cream on and shave. Not one single cut. Message received.

22. NERF FOOTBALL

Remember when you got your first nerf football? You were like, "Hey this is cheap. This isn't a real football." And then you decided to play with it anyway. And right away you started to have fun. And then your brother threw the nerf right at your head and you ducked but it hit you anyway. But it didn't hurt at all. And you started to think, "Thank goodness this isn't a real football!" Remember that?

23. SUPER DRY SPEED STICK

The first thing I noticed when I hit puberty was that I started to smell—bad. I guess I wasn't the only one who noticed 'cause one day a stick of Super Dry Anti-Perspirant appeared in my locker. There was note, too. "From your friends. Please use it." I do. And now I don't smell bad at all. Aren't friends great? *(Looking in his locker)* Oh no, it's a bottle of mouthwash.

24. RAVE CLOTHING

I'm hip. I'm happening. I'm the man! I've got on a Rave shirt. Some Rave pants. And check out these cool Rave socks. I'm stylin' now! Rave. It's just another word for cool.

A lot of commercials just have one line of dialogue. Here are some one-liners to practice with. The best way to work on them is to pick any product (cookies, soda pop, etc.) and use the one-liner to express how you feel about the product.

25. Wow!

    All right!

    Fantastic!

    Tremendous!

    Magnificent!

    Excellent!

26. It's nice and gooey!

    Yum, yum!

    Delicious!

27. Mom!

    Yes I can!

    Ow!

    Uh-oh!

28. Smells great!

    Tastes great!

29. Mom, what's for dinner?

30. I feel sick!

    Ow! My head hurts.

    Mom! My stomach hurts

31. That's great, Dad!

    Good job, Mom!

101 Commercials

Some commercials can be very silly. MTV and Nickelodeon are full of goofy commercials. Here are some examples of those kinds of commercials but remember, just because they're silly, doesn't mean you don't take performing them seriously. Practice these so that your silliness sells the product!

32. MOCHA COFFEE

Are you always falling asleep in history class? Are you exhausted after lunch? Are you too pooped to—you know? Well, that was me until I discovered Mocha Coffee from Mexico. Made with a special blend of coffee beans and Mexican jumping beans. It's so strong it has me on the move. I have so much energy now I just broke the world's record for most jumping jacks. *(Do two jumping jacks)* Three thousand and one. Three thousand and two. Get Mocha from Mexico. And you will have energy, too!

33. MUSTARD

(A girl putting on lipstick)
Yuck! My lipstick tastes like a gas station.
And it rubs off so easily.
So now I use mustard.
It stains your lips and tastes good, too!

34. POST-IT NOTES

Tired of buying new clothes?
As soon as you buy them they go out of style.
That's why I wear Post-it Notes!
The sticky little sheets of paper that stick to your body.
They come in tons of great colors.

cont. next page

I'm never out of style.
When putting them on just be careful not to miss a spot.
Post-it Notes, today's fashion today.

35.   CARROTS

I've always hated vegetables.
Until last week when just as I was about to take a big test,
I went blind.
I couldn't see my hand in front of my face.
Immediately I was taken to the hospital and given an injection of
carrot juice.
Now I can practically see through walls. *(Looks at wall)*
Hey put some clothes on in there!
Carrots saved my life.
Announcer - Brought to you by the national carrot advisory board.

36.   JOHNSON'S NO MORE TANGLES SHAMPOO

Brush, brush, ow.
Brush, brush, ooow—
I wish my mom would buy Johnson's No More Tangles shampoo,
before I go BALD!

37.   SHERMAN CARPET CLEANERS

Kid   - Mom, I just threw up.
Mom - Oh honey. Are you okay?
Kid   - *(Mean)* I just hurled. Do you feel good when you hurl?
Mom - Where did you do it?
Kid   - On the sofa?
Mom - The new sofa?
Kid   - But don't worry, most of it got on the new carpet.
Announcer - Sherman's Carpet Cleaners. No jobs too messy for us.

38.   JELL-O PUDDING

Kid #1   -   Ooo, are you going to eat that?
Kid #2   -   Yeah.
Kid #1   -   I know someone who ate that kind of pudding
             and died.
Kid #2   -   He did not.
Kid #1   -   Did too. His tongue fell off and his face
             turned puffy, purple and exploded!
Kid #2   -   Really?
Kid #1   -   Give me that pudding so I can throw it away.
Kid #2   -   Thanks for saving my life. See ya later.
(Kid #2 exits. Kid #1 starts eating the pudding)
Kid #1   -   MMMMMMM this is good.

Announcer - Jell-O Pudding. We turn your kids into liars.

39.   UCLA MEDICAL CENTER

Last month I fainted at soccer practice. My dad, the coach, took
me to UCLA Medical Center. The doctor said I had a brain tumor
as big as a baseball. Which is too bad because I play soccer. The
next day they cut my head open and took the baseball out. Now
I'm I feeling a lot better. If I didn't keep walking into walls you
would never know I was even sick! Thank you UCLA!

40.   CAN OF WORMS

Whenever I come home from school, the first thing I do is rush to
the kitchen and get a Can of Worms. Mom knows how I love to
put those squishy little bugs in my mouth. And because worms
are 100% protein, they are good for me too! So try Can of
Worms today.

41. DIRT

My teeth used to be white as snow. But all the kids made fun of me. They called me Little Miss Perfect. So now I brush my teeth with Dirt. It goes right to my gums staining my whole mouth an ugly brown color. I know it doesn't look good but at least now the kids have stopped picking on me. Brush with Dirt. You won't be sorry.

42. ODOR EATERS

My dad's feet stink. It's impossible to grow any plants in our house cause my dad's feet kill them. So for Christmas we got him Odor Eaters. He just puts them in his shoes and the bad smell goes away. Now we just need to find something for his breath.

43. ZIT BE GONE

I woke up this morning with a huge zit on my shoulder. It was so big it looked like I had an extra head. My sister heard me screaming and rushed in with a bottle of Zit Be Gone. Ten times stronger than Oxy 10, it went right to work. Within hours, my zit was gone. Of course, so was my shoulder. But hey, at least I don't have any more zits.

Public Service Announcements are another form of commercial. They are usually about very serious subjects. When you perform them, try to be as believable as possible.

44. SUICIDE

There was this girl at school named Katie. I saw her everyday in class but I never talked to her. She was—different. Her clothes and stuff weren't—well they were weird. Once she wore this cool purple jacket. I was going to tell her I liked it, but I never did. Today the principal announced Katie committed suicide. I should have said something to her. Maybe we could have been friends.

45. CHILD ABUSE

Parents should never hit their kids. Violence never solves anything. I mean come on, pick on someone your own size. If you know of anyone who uses violence to solve their problems, call Oasis at 555-6767. I did and they saved my life.

46. CANCER

My dad hadn't had a check-up in 5 years. Mom and I bugged him so much that he finally went to see a doctor. It turned out he had colon cancer. But lucky for us they found it early. Now my dad is okay. See a doctor for a yearly checkup. It's better late than never.

47. PBS

Remember when you were little and you watched Sesame Street and Barney? Well those great shows are on PBS. And PBS has no commercials. It's supported by viewers like you. So if you want other people to grow up watching Big Bird and that purple dinosaur, call your local PBS station today and make a donation.

48. VOTE

In some countries people are put to death for speaking their mind. In some countries, an opinion is a dangerous thing. Some countries have had the same dictators for the last thirty years. Vote. It's not just a privilege. It's freedom.

49. BOYS CLUB

My dad died when I was little. My mom did the best she could raising me and my brothers. But sometimes we were wild. You know in the way boys can be. So she signed us up with the Boys Club of America. There we met men that helped us become men too. If you know a kid who needs help, Boys Club could be the answer.

50. DRUGS

They said it was cool. They said it would make me feel better. They said I would never have to worry again. They didn't say I would get addicted. Drugs. It's what they don't say that can kill you.

51. DRUNK

Amy said, "Don't worry about it. I'm not drunk." So I got in the car with her, Kelly and Kate. The next thing I knew, I was thrown from the car into a ditch. But at least I lived. Kelly and Kate weren't so lucky. And now Amy wishes she were dead. I wish I *had* worried.

52. CANCER

There used to be smallpox. There used to be polio. There used to be Cancer. Well there still is cancer. But maybe someday it will vanish like smallpox and polio. Give to the Cancer Foundation. Getting rid of disease is hard. But not impossible.

53. PREGNANT

I thought I was old enough. But I wasn't. I thought I was responsible. But I'm not. I never thought I would be a mommy so soon. But I am. Think before you act.

54. SPAYED/NEUTERED

I love my cat Daisy. I got her at the pound. As soon as I saw her in her little cage, I knew I had to bring her home. But first we had to have her spayed so she couldn't have kittens. After going to the pound, I know there are already enough cats in this world. Have your animals spayed or neutered today.

55. HUNGER SOCIETY

Every minute someone in the world dies of hunger. Give to the Hunger Society. We help millions of people each day find a meal. If you give a dollar a day, by the end of the year you will have helped us feed over a hundred people. Give. We are talking about a life here.

A lot of commercials have more than one person in them. Work on these two-person commercials so you'll be prepared.

56.   FIG NEWTONS - #1

Kid one - *(Eating)* Umm.
Kid two - Boy that looks good.
Kid one - It is good.
Kid two - Do you think I could have a bite?
Kid one - No!
Kid two - Please.
Kid one - Sorry. *(He pops the whole cookie in his mouth)*
         All Gone.

Announcer - Fig Newtons. They make your kid selfish.

57.   FIG NEWTONS - #2

Kid one - *(Eating)* Umm.
Kid two - Boy that looks good.
Kid one - It is good.
Kid two - Do you think I could have a bite?
Kid one - I guess.
Kid Two - *(Grabbing the cookie and putting the whole thing in her mouth)* Wow it is good.
Kid one - Thanks a lot.

Announcer - Fig Newtons. They make your kid devious.

58.   M & M's

Kid one - *(Counting M & M's)* One, two, three—
Kid two - *(Walking up)* How many M & M's do you have?
Kid one - Seven. Three plain, two almond, one peanut
          and one peanut butter.
Kid two - *(Grabbing them and putting them in his mouth)*
          Now you have none.

59.   LOW FAT RICE-A-RONI - #1

Kid one - What's wrong?
Kid two - My mom is making meatloaf again.
Kid one - Oh no.
Kid two - And guess what she's serving with it?
Kid one - Don't tell me.
Kid two - Potatoes. With sour cream.
Kid one - Boy, talk about fat. Hey, my mom's serving new
          low fat Rice-a-Roni. I'll ask her if you can eat over.
Kid two - Great! I thank you. And my waistline thanks
          you too!

60.   RICE-A-RONI - #2

Kid one - Sally, have you gained some weight?
Kid two - Yeah, my mom is making a lot of fattening foods
          nowadays.
Kid one - Does she know about fat-free Rice-a-Roni?
Kid two - Yeah, but she says if something is fat free it
          doesn't have any taste.
Kid one - Tell her to try Rice-a-Roni. It's got so much
          taste, it makes my mouth tingle.

61.   MCDONALDS

Kid   - Look Mom, no matter what you say I'm not
        going to clean my room.
Mom - No matter what?
Kid   - No matter what.
Mom - *(As she's leaving)* Okay then, no McDonalds'
        french fries for you.
Kid   - Wait Mom, I need to borrow a vacuum
        cleaner!

Here are some commercials selling vegetables and vegetable products. Memorize them. *(Don't ad lib. Memorize them <u>exactly</u> as they appear on the page.)* Then perform them for members of your family. Make them natural. Use hand props if you want. Have fun.

62. CORN

I used to hate vegetables. Until I discovered Mrs. Warner's Frozen Corn. Just put it in the microwave and a minute later you have a tasty treat. Mrs. Warner's Frozen Corn comes creamed or on the cob. Get yours at your grocer's freezer today.

63. EGGPLANT

I don't get it. Is it an egg or is it a plant? And why is it purple? Whatever it is, it tastes great. Eggplant, I don't know what it is. But it's yummy.

64. APPLES

(Singing) Crunch. Crunch. Crunch. Crunch. I love to Crunch. Crunch. Crunch. Crunch. I love to Munch. Munch. Munch. Munch. Put an apple in your lunch. Lunch. Lunch. Lunch. I could eat a bunch—

Announcer - Put an apple in your child's lunch. It will make them sing.

65. CARROTS

My mom said, "Eat your carrots. They're good for you." I was like, "Naa". Then she said, "But Bugs Bunny eats carrots. " But I was like, "So? He's a rabbit!" Then she said, "They'll improve your eye-

cont. next page

sight." Then I said, "Will I be able to see through walls like Superman?" And she said, "Naa. Just try them. Please." So I did. And they were good. She should've just said they tasted good. It would have saved her a lot of trouble.

66.   WATERMELON

Today my mother brought home a watermelon from the store. I've always hated watermelon mainly because of the seeds. Every time you take a bite, your mouth is full of seeds. But guess what? Our watermelon didn't have seeds. My mom said, "They're the new, seedless watermelons from Hawley Farms." I took one bite. And all I tasted was melon. I have only one question. If there are no seeds, how do you grow them?

67.   CELERY

My grandmother thinks she is so smart. She knows I hate vegetables. So for a snack she gave me a plate of celery. I told her I wasn't hungry. But then she put out a jar of peanut butter and dipped a piece of celery in it. Well, I love peanut butter. So I picked up the celery and tasted a little bite. Wow! Maybe grandma is smarter than I thought.

68.   GRAPES

It's hot outside. Real hot. So I went to the freezer to get a popsicle. But my brother had eaten the last one. So now I was mad *and* hot. Then I noticed someone had accidentally put the grapes in the freezer. Well, it's better than nothing. Did you know frozen grapes taste like popsicles? Well, I didn't. I ate them all. Now my brother is the one who is mad.

69.   BANANAS

I love bananas. I could eat them for every meal. My dad said if I eat one more banana I'm going to turn into a monkey. That's silly. Watch. *(He peels the banana)* Nice and ripe the way I like them. *(He takes a big bite)* See, nothing happened. *(He starts making monkey noises)* Uh-oh! I think my dad was right.

70.   ORANGES

You've seen those commercials that say, "Inside this orange is a glass of paradise". Well, I don't know about that, but if it says Florida on the outside, then I know it tastes sweet on the inside.
Announcer - Florida Oranges. A glass of paradise.

71.   ONIONS

Every time my mom chops up onions, she cries. I tell her I'm sorry onions are my favorite food. She says, *(a big cry)*, "That's okay. I just want you to be happy." What a great mom.

72.   PEAS

Kids of America. Over the last week, I've received a million letters telling me the best way to eat peas. Some kids say a fork. But when I tried that they fell off. Some kids say a spoon. But then I only got a little bit of peas at a time. Then I discovered the two handed system. That way you can eat as many peas as you want before your dad gets hold of them.

Here are some more commercials you can use to practice. The more you practice the better chance you have of being ready when that big audition comes your way.

73. SMORES CEREAL

Marshmallows are my favorite food. If my parent would let me, I would eat them all the time. But Mom says I have to eat something besides marshmallows. So she bought me Smores Cereal. Just pour on the milk and it's like having marshmallows for breakfast. Now if she would just let me make marshmallow sandwiches.

74. ITALIAN SURPRISE SPAGHETTI SAUCE

My little sister likes everything simple. Hamburgers with just meat and a bun. Pizza with just cheese. And spaghetti without the sauce. But then Mom got Italian Surprise Spaghetti Sauce. My little sister took one bite and —surprise! She liked it!

75. Orville Redenbacher's Smart Pop Movie Theater
      Pop Corn. *(Try version A, then B. Make them very different.)*

A. Orville Redenbacher's Smart Pop Movie Theater Pop Corn. For such a funny name, it sure does taste good!

B. Is it Orville Redenbacher's Smart Pop Movie Theater Pop Corn or is it Orville Redenbacher's Movie Theater Smart Pop Pop Corn? Whatever it's called, it sure tastes good!

76. HAMBURGER HELPER

My favorite food is Hamburger Helper. It's a good thing 'cause it's all my dad can cook. He says all you have to do is brown a pound of hamburger and then just add water and what's in the box. That's so simple even a kid could make dinner. Just don't tell my dad. It's bad enough I have to do the dishes.

77. FROSTED FLAKES

The best thing about Frosted Flakes cereal is the toy in the bottom of the box. *(Opening the box of cereal)* Look, a yo-yo! *(Tasting the cereal)* Wait a minute. Maybe the toy is the second best thing.

78. CHIPS AHOY
(A kid dressed up like a scientist. He/she has chocolate all over his/her face.)

After careful analysis I have determined than Chips Ahoy chocolate chip cookies have twice as much chocolate as the other leading brand. At least I think they do. But I could be wrong. Maybe I better test them again. *(The kid shoves a cookie in his/her mouth.)*

79. DOMINOS

I love babysitting my little brother. Because whenever I do, my mom pays me by buying me a pizza from Dominos. *(Looking at the crib)* Hey, buddy, look what I got. Your favorite. Pepperoni pizza. Oh, look at him smile. He is so cute. Coochy, coochy coo. *(The baby grabs the piece of pizza)* Hey, that's my piece. Hey, give it back. Okay, you can have it but next time I'm ordering anchovies. He hates anchovies.

80. BURGER KING

My Grandma is always going on about how tough it was when she was little. Yeah right. So what if she had to sleep in a log cabin. I could do that. And so what if she had to walk to school in the snow. I could easily do that. And so what if she never got to eat out because there were no restaurants. I could—wait a minute. There was no Burger King? Oh poor Grandma. How did she stand it?

81. TACO BELL

What do you call spicy ground beef mixed with refried beans, lettuce, tomatoes, cheese, spicy sauce, sour cream, onions, rolled together in a warm tortilla? Well, Taco Bell calls it a Burrito Supreme. I call it delicious.

82. SNACKWELL COOKIES

My mom never buys us cookies because she says they make her fat. Does that seem fair? Not to us kids. But then she discovered new Snackwell chocolate chip cookies. They taste great so we're happy. And they are low in fat, so Mom's happy too.

83. HEINZ KETCHUP

Eating a hamburger without Heinz ketchup is like—well I don't know what it's like but it's not good. Heinz Ketchup tastes good. And makes everything it touches taste good too.

84.   ONE

This is supposed to be a diet soda? It tastes like a—well it doesn't taste like a diet soda. It tastes sweet without the aftertaste. Are you sure this is a diet soda? *(Taking a big drink)* I know why they call it One. Because from now on it's the only one I'm going to be drinking.

85.   ACME FINANCIAL INVESTMENTS
     (A kid looking in a crystal ball)

Four. Eleven. Thirty-three. Seventy-two. No wait. Maybe three. Eleven. Thirty-nine. Seventy-two. No, its thirty-seven. Seventy-five. Or is that a seventy-eight?

Announcer - Picking the winning lottery numbers isn't easy. But picking a financial adviser is. Acme Financial Investments. We'll make you lucky.

86.   POST OFFICE

My grandfather collects stamps. For my birthday he gave me my own stamp collecting book. He bought it right at the post office. And look, it has a lot of stamps already in it. Here's one with baseball players on it. And here's one with an astronaut. And look, here's one with Elvis. Someday I'm going to have it full like my grandfather's book. Oh look, here comes the postman. I better get busy.

87. TYLENOL JR.

When my head hurts, my mom gives me Tylenol Jr. It's gentle on my stomach and gets rid of my headache. Aren't mom's smart?

88. KLEENEX - #1

Whenever I get a cold, I only blow my nose with Kleenex. Ah-choo! Mom, I need some Kleenex!

KLEENEX- #2

My mom has got a cold. My dad has got a cold. And now I have a cold. Thank goodness we have Kleenex.

89. EAGLE AIR

When my grandma invited me to visit her in Alaska, I was a little nervous. I had never been on a plane before. But my mom told me not to worry, I was flying on Eagle Air. The safest airline in the sky. And it's perfect for kids. Every seat has its own video game system. And the stewardess served candy. When I got to Alaska, my grandma had to drag me off the plane. Eagle Air. For kids, there is no better airplane.

90. PACIFIC GAS

I asked my mom why we cook with gas instead of electricity. She said gas is cheaper and cooks your food faster, too. She said with the money she saves, we can go to the waterpark this summer. And guess what? The waterpark heats the water with gas.

91. KISS-FM

I'm tired of turning on the radio and only hearing commercials. On KISS-FM they play more music than commercials. So if you're ready to hear your favorite bands, turn on KISS-FM. They play what you want to hear.

92. BASKIN ROBBINS

I'm here at Baskin Robbins trying to break the world record for eating the world's biggest sundae. You see, for a limited time only, Baskin Robbins will make you a giant sundae using any of their 32 flavors. And for only $1.99. *(Showing the sundae)* So come back next week and see if I break the record.

93. I CAN'T BELIEVE IT'S NOT BUTTER

I think my mom is going crazy. She keeps walking around the kitchen saying, "I can't believe it's not butter." She keeps saying it over and over again. I'm starting to get worried. *(Picking up package)* Hey, what's this? *(Tastes it)* Wow, I can't believe it's not butter. I can't believe it's not butter. Oh, no, I'm starting to do it too.

94. SMART POP

One of the best things about going to the movies is popcorn. Well, now you can have that great movie popcorn taste right in your own home with Smart Pop. I just pop it in the microwave and—POP I have popcorn. Smart Pop. It's like going to the movies.

95. KMART

My best friend Allie is always borrowing my pens. And the worse part is she always loses them before she gives them back. It finally made me so mad, I told my mom. She said not to worry. Kmart is having a sale. Ten pens for only a dollar. So we went and bought twenty dollars worth. We had to. Allie is coming over to study.

96. PRINGLES

My mom goes to the grocery store and brings home some potato chips in a can. A can! I tell her "potato chips do not come in a can." She says, "Try 'em". I did. And you know what? They were the best potato chips I've ever eaten. I wonder who thought to put potato chips in a can?

Announcer: Pringles. That great potato chips taste—in a can.

97. OREOS

Everybody has their favorite way of eating oreos. Some people eat the cookie first. Some people eat the middle. Me? I just pop the whole cookie in my mouth.

Announcer: Oreos. They taste good no matter how you
               eat them.

98. VOLKSWAGON

For my birthday my dad brings home one of those new Volkswagon beetles. It was so cool. I couldn't believe he bought it for me. He said, "Before you were born, my first car was a Volkswagon beetle. And I loved it. And now I love you. So I want you to have the best. And the best is a Volkswagon."

99. SALSA

When I'm planning a party, I make sure I get lots of Pace Salsa. The great thing about Pace Thick and Chunky Salsa is that is goes with everything: chips, burritos, even eggs. And it come mild or hot. Salsa. It's the perfect party food.

100. OXY WASH

I have oily skin. So everyday I wash with Oxy Wash. It's strong enough to get rid of the oil. And gentle enough to leave my skin nice and soft. And after my wash, I use Oxy 10 on my problem areas. If you want clear skin, you have to use the right products. Oxy Wash keeps me clean.

101. CARMEX

When my lips are chapped, I use Carmex. Soft lips are important.
You never know when you might need them.

+101. TOMATOES

My mother says Tomatoes (TOH-MAY-TOHS). My dad says
Tomatoes (TAH-MAY-TOHS). I say, "Whatever you call them, can I
have some more?"

Getting

an

Agent

Have you been practicing your commercials? Can you perform them smoothly and naturally? Can you memorize quickly? If you answered *yes*, then you are ready for the next big step in your commercial career: getting an agent.

Booking a national commercial is nearly impossible without having an agent. Oh yeah, it happens every once-in-a-while like when Oscar Mayer travels the country looking for a kid who can sing, "I wish I were an Oscar Mayer Wiener." But those opportunities are rare.

So how do you get an agent? Well, it is not as difficult as most people think. First you have to know that agents *need* talented kids. If agents don't have good kids, they don't make any money. And since the kids they do have are constantly growing, the agents are always on the look-out for their newest star. Who knows, that could be you.

Now before I tell you how to get an agent, let me tell you what an agent is and what an agent is not.

An agent is —

1. Someone who submits you for commercial auditions.
2. Negotiates your salary when you book the commercial.

Getting an Agent

For those two things, they take 10% of the money you make from the commercial job.

What an agent doesn't do —

1. Get jobs for you. If an agent promises you jobs, then they aren't being honest with you.
2. Take money from you *before* you get a job. If the agent asks for money before you get a job—run! They are not really an agent.
3. Takes more than 10% of your money from a commercial job.

Okay, so how do you get in touch with an agent?

Write them a letter.

Isn't that simple? All you have to do is write them a letter. In the back of this book I have enclosed addresses of some of the best kids commercial agents in the country. With your letter, you need to enclose a picture of youself. *(I'll go into that more later)* If the agent is looking for your type, they will call you and set up an audition.

Sounds easy, doesn't it?

Here are two examples of letters you can write.

Sample Agent Letter #1

Date
Agent's Name
Agent's Company
Agent's Address

Dear (Agent's Name):

My name is Lisa Michelle and I'm looking for an agent. I read in the book *24-Carat Commercials for Kids* that you are one of the best agents in *(insert the name of your town)*. Well guess what? I'm one of the best young actors in *(insert town)*. I recently played the lead in a production of Annie at my school. It was a big hit. I also have been studying acting and dance for a number of years. How about letting me come in and do a commercial for you?

See you soon,

Lisa Michelle

This letter works because it comes right from the mouth of the kid. It's honest, short, and to-the-point.

Here is a letter that a parent wrote.

Sample Agent Letter #2

Date
Agent's Name
Agent's Company
Agent's Address

Dear (Agent's Name):

My son, Collin, is currently looking for commercial representation. For the last couple of months, he has been driving us crazy practicing commercials from the book *24-Carat Commercials For Kids*. After listening to him endlessly, I feel that he is ready to be on TV.

How about letting him come in and do a commercial for you?

See you soon,

Susan Hastings
(Collin's mother)

The parent letter works because it is funny and, like Lisa's letter, it quickly gets to-the-point.

Now it's time to write your own letter.

EXERCISE: WRITE YOUR INTRODUCTION LETTER TO AN AGENT

Tell them you are looking for a commercial agent. Then tell them a little bit about yourself and ask to come in and do a commercial for them. Keep your letter short.

Now, what happens when you visit an agent?

After an agent has read your letter and seen your picture and decides to bring you in for a meeting, then what happens? Well this is where your weeks of practicing commercials comes in. Most agent meetings go something like this:

Agent walks into the waiting room where Stephanie and her parents have been sitting.

Agent   -   Hello. I'm Allison Westmoreland. You must be Stephanie?

Stephanie -   Yes. Nice to meet you.

Agent   -   Why don't you come on back to my office. *(To Stephanie's parents)* I'll come and get you in a couple of minutes.

The agent takes Stephanie into her office.

Agent   - Have a seat. So—you want to be
              on television?

Stephanie - Absolutely. I love to act. I've been in
              a couple of plays. Last year I played Becky
              Sawyer in The Story of Tom Sawyer
              at my school. And this year I did two
              different plays at my church.

Agent   - So, you can sing?

Stephanie - Well, not very good. But I can dance. I've
              taken ballet, jazz and hip hop. I can even tap.

Agent   - Really? Last week we were casting a
              McDonald's commercial and we were
              looking for a girl who could tap. Too bad
              I didn't know you then.

Stephanie - Bummer. Would you like to see a
              commercial I've been working on?

Agent   - Oh sure.

Stephanie - I have five memorized.

Agent   - I only need to see one.

Stephanie - So would you rather see Oreos, Dorritos,
              Burger King, Coke or Spaghetti?

Agent   - You choose.

(Stephanie performs her commercial. She does great.)

Agent   - Fantastic. Let me go get your parents.

———

I have sent hundreds of kids to agents and most of
the time, this is exactly how the interview goes.

Let's go through all the things Stephanie did right.

1. *Stephanie was nice and courteous with the agent.*
   Remember the agent has to like you to represent you.

2. *When the agent suggested that Stephanie leave her parents in the lobby, she did not complain.*
   Most agents want to see the actor alone. They want to see how you handle yourself *without* your parent's help. During auditions and on the set, it's you, not them, who has to be ready to do the job. Also, parents tend to dominate the interview. Do yourself a favor and leave them in the lobby.

3. *Stephanie was very talkative.*
   Every time the agent asked her a question, she not only answered it but she <u>kept talking</u>. When you are talkative, it shows that you have confidence. Of course it is also important to be a good listener. Just remember the old phrase, "Kids should be seen and not heard" does *not* apply to kid actors.

4. *Stephanie told the truth.*
   She knew she couldn't sing, so she told the truth. Don't lie to your agent. I once had a kid who lied to his agent. He told her he could skateboard when he couldn't. The agent sent him on a Pepsi audition where he had to skateboard. The kid broke his arm.

5. *Stephanie turned all negatives into positives.*
    The agent asked Stephanie if she could sing.
    Stephanie said, "Well, not very good." But then she
    went on to tell the agent about the things <u>she</u>
    <u>could do,</u> like dance. Agents need kids with many
    skills. Stephanie scored points here by showing the
    agent she is versatile.

6. *Stephanie asked to do a commercial.*
    After Stephanie was sure that the agent liked her,
    she offered to do a commercial. Remember, the
    bottom line is: commercials are what the agent will
    be representing you for. So Stephanie, after having
    worked for weeks, felt confident in her ability to
    perform. The agent was impressed.

EXERCISE - GET ONE OF YOUR PARENTS TO INTERVIEW YOU

Follow Stephanie's example by:

- ° Being nice and courteous.
- ° Being talkative.
- ° Answering every question with a full, complete
  answer.
- ° Tell them about your many skills.
- ° Volunteer to do a commercial.

Interview your kid by asking him/her the following questions:

1.   What grade are you in?

2.   What school do you go to?

3.   What are your favorite subjects and why?

4.   What subjects do you hate and why?

5.   Why do you want to be an actor?

6.   What kind of acting have you done before?

7.   Do you have any special skills?

8.   Tell me about yourself.

9.   Is there any part of acting you don't like?

10. How are your grades in school?

11. Is there anything else I should know about you?

12. Are there any kinds of commercials you would not do?

How did you do? You might need to practice this several times to get it flowing so that you say what you want to say and don't mess up. Don't wait until you are in the agent's office to think about these questions and worry about how to answer them. A good actor is ready! Be prepared.

A note on rejection.

No matter how much you practice, sometimes an agent just won't accept you. It could be they already have enough kids your age. It could be they already have enough blondes (redheads, kids with braces, etc.) It could be that the agent doesn't think you are ready to go out on a real audition.

It could be that the agent is WRONG.

I have seen tons of kids be rejected by various agents. Sometimes for the stupidest reasons. And those same kids have gone on to have a wonderful commercial career. One kid I knew got rejected eleven times in a row. The twelfth agent accepted him and now he has done 23 national commercials! Agents can be wrong. Remember that.

If you are rejected, don't let it get you down. Just write another letter to another agent. Believe in yourself. And keep practicing your commercials. It never hurts to try. It just hurts to quit.

Pictures,

Résumés,

Work Permits

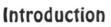

& The

Commercial

Audition

I can't tell you enough how important good pictures are to your career. No wait, I'm sorry. Forget good pictures. You need GREAT pictures.

EXERCISE: REPEAT OUT LOUD TEN TIMES

"I will get great pictures. I will get great pictures!"

You think I'm kidding? I have seen a girl get a national commercial that paid her $20,000. And she didn't even have to audition. The director cast her based on her picture alone. HE DIDN'T EVEN MEET HER FIRST! He just looked at her picture and cast her on the spot. Now do you understand how important great pictures are?

What is a commercial picture? Commercial pictures are always:

1. Black and white
2. 8 inches x 10 inches

I recommend that you have your name printed on the front of the picture. It's also a good idea to have your agent's name on the front as well. Some people prefer to have a border around their picture, while others prefer the picture borderless. I have seen pictures with a matte and glossy finish. It doesn't matter. Just make sure your pictures are GREAT.

What do you wear in a commercial picture?

I've asked one of Hollywood's most experienced photographers, Karl Preston, to answer this question for you. Karl started his career as a model traveling all over the world. Then he took up photography and quickly became one of the industry's best headshot photographers. Karl is also the author of the popular book, *Modelmania*. So Karl, what do you wear in a commercial headshot?

Karl Preston:

"Well Chambers I'm glad you asked. Like you said before, agents and casting directors see hundreds of head shots weekly. So a GREAT headshot is very important. You want to stand out in a crowd (of photographs).

Rule #1: Colors don't matter

Try to see everything in tones instead of colors. Commercial shots are black & white—light tones, medium tones and dark tones. I prefer whites (lights) and blacks (darks) to create a higher contrast on film, rather than boring gray tones. Sometimes lighter tones make a nice contrast on dark complexion skin and hair, while darker tones achieve the same purpose for a light complexion skin and hair.

Rule #2:   Avoid busy clothes

Try to avoid busy patterns such as stripes and plaids. They generally make a photograph too busy and distract from the subject—you. Big logos, like NIKE or ADIDAS should also be avoided for the same reason.

Rule #3:   Keep it casual

Keep it fairly casual and simple for both girls & boys. On the casual side, jeans and a T-shirt are great. Maybe even a pair of overalls, a jean jacket, a sweater (all worn separately of course). Khakis pants, a polo shirt or a button-up shirt for boys. Maybe a cute blouse or a one-piece sun dress for girls. You know, clothes that you would wear on your first day back to school. The Gap and Eddie Bauer have great clothes in this style.

Rule #4:   Don't dress up

Look like you are going to school, not church. Avoid upscale wardrobe for both boys and girls. Suits and fufu dresses will make you look like little adults instead of kids.

Rule #5:   Be unique

Every boy and every girl obviously has his/her own unique quality and physical characteristics. The parents' job, along with the photographer, and the agent (if he/she has one), is to define the boy or girl's 'type' in relation to the film and TV industry and produce 'winning' head-shots. A boy with the right look could very well be cast as a bully, therefore he should shoot in the appropriate T-shirt and jeans along with the right attitude and expression. If your girl is more of a tomboy, shoot her in overalls or a jean jacket. If not, then shoot her with small, nondistracting ribbons.

And the most important thing required for a great commercial shot: **a smile!** Casting directors are always looking for a bright shining face. Most kids look better with a smile."

Thank you Karl. That was great!

Pictures, Résumés and Work Permits

A résumé is a single sheet of paper stapled to the back of your picture. An actor's résumé is never more than a single sheet of paper!

What is on a résumé?

The Actor's name	
Contact number	Usually this is the agent's phone number
The Agent's Name	
Hair color	
Eye color	
Height	
Weight	
Experience	This includes any plays, television or films that the actor has performed in.
Training	Listing of all classes taken. Include acting, dancing and any musical instruments you can play.
Special Skills	A list of everything that you can do. Include sports played, accents that you can imitate. Can you juggle or hackysax? Then put it down.

Now here are two examples of résumés and four examples of commercial headshots. Yours should look great, like these!

COLLIN HASTING
615-555-3215

Height: 3'5"
Hair: Sandy Brown
Weight: 50 lbs.
Eyes: Blue
Date of Birth: 1/5/93

PLAYS

Veggie Tales   Junior Asparagus   Baptist Church
Beanstalk Jack   Cow   Pegram Elemen.

SPECIAL SKILLS

T-Ball, Soccer, Lego Master, Checkers, Singing, Beginning
Piano, Joke telling, Godzilla Watching

Scarlett Pomers
SAG/AFTRA

HAIR: Strawberry   EYES: Blue   HEIGHT: 4'1"

tgi/YOUTH
6300 Wilshire Blvd.
Los Angeles, CA 90048
(213) 852-9555

FILM (Partial List)	ROLE	DIRECTOR
Happy, Texas	Lead (Jency)	Mark Illsley
Mighty Joe Young	Featured (Charlotte)	Ron Underwood/Disney
Baby Geniuses	V/O Lead	Bob Clark/Crystal Sky
Slappy and the Stinkers	Lead (Lucy)	Barnet Kellman/Tri-Star
The Babysitter's Club	Supporting (Suzi)	Melanie Mayron/Columbia
Life on Mars	Lead (Jesse)	Varoun Arora/AFI
Indictment	Featured (Sara)	Mick Jackson/HBO

TELEVISION		
Martial Law	Co-Star	CBS
Star Trek Voyager	Recurring (Naomi)	UPN
One Saturday Morning	Co-Star	ABC
America's Wildest Kids	Co-Star	UPN
A Visit With Santa	Starring	Direct to Video
The Jeff Foxworthy Show	Co-Star	NBC
Touched By An Angel	Guest Star	CBS Ent.
Step By Step	Co-Star	ABC
Simon Said What (Pilot)	Series Regular	Nickelodeon/Lynch Ent.
Skwids (Pilot)	Recurring	Nickelodeon
Secret World of Alex Mack	Guest Star	Nickelodeon
Later w/Greg Kinnear	Featured	NBC

COMMERCIALS	List Available On Request	

RADIO		
Adventures in Odyssey	Recurring (Sarah)	Focus On The Family Prod.

THEATRE (Partial List)		
Ruthless	Lead (Tina Denmark)	Morgan-Wixson Theatre
I'll Be Home For Christmas	Lead (Sandy)	Reseda Baptist Church
Someone To Count On	Lead (Marci)	St. Paul's Church

TRAINING
Dance: American National Academy of Performing Arts
Voice: Mark Vogel (private coaching)

SPECIAL SKILLS
SINGING: Dance, Accents (British, Southern, Valley Girl), Loves Aimals,
Horseback Riding (English and Western)

Visit Scarlett's website at: http://surf.to/pomers

Tape Available

Andrew McFarland

Lauren Schaffel

Saroya Whatley

Travis Tedford

Pictures, Résumés & Work Permit

Now that you have your pictures and résumé finished, you need to think about a work permit. Have your parents/guardian read the next few pages.

FOR PARENTS/GUARDIANS:

If your kid is to work in the entertainment industry, you must research information on the state labor laws and education requirements. Usually your agent will give you the proper information. Each state has different requirements. Some states ban kids from working at all unless they receive a waiver. Others let the kids work if they receive permission from their school principal. Like I said, most agents will know what rules apply to you. But it never hurts to check with the local authorities anyway.

FOR PARENTS WHO LIVE IN CALIFORNIA:

For a kid to work in California he/she must obtain an Entertainment Work Permit. Here is how you do that.

1. In order for your child to obtain a valid California Work Permit, she/he must have and maintain a "C" average in school.

2. Obtain a yellow work permit application card from your local Entertainment Permit office.

3. If he/she is in elementary school, have his/her <u>teacher</u> sign the work permit. If he/she is in secondary school, the <u>principal, vice principal, counselor, dean etc.</u> must sign the work permit. If school is not in session, include a copy of the most recent report card.

4. Return the signed form and a self-addressed stamped envelope to the Entertainment Permit office. You will be

rewarded with a work permit good for six months in approximately three weeks. If you need to have a work permit more quickly than that, you can go to the permit office personally. But check on their hours of operation before you go. They are not always open to walk-up applications.

I recommend that you get a work permit as soon as you get an agent. I have known a couple of young actors who signed with an agent on Monday morning, went to an audition on Monday afternoon, and started working on Tuesday morning. Lucky for them they already had their work permit. Don't let your kid down. Get his/her work permit today.

CA DIVISIONS OF LABOR STANDARDS ENFORCEMENT OFFICES:
5555 California Ave., Suite 200, Bakersfield, CA 93309
619 Second Street, Room 109, Eureka, CA 95501
107 South Broadway, Room 5015, Los Angeles, CA 90012
1204 "E" Street, Marysville, CA 95901
360 22nd Street, Room 500, Oakland, CA 94612
770 East Shaw Avenue, Suite 227 Fresno, CA 93704
300 Oceangate, Room 302, Long Beach, CA 90802
2115 Akard Avenue, Room 17, Redding, CA 96001
2424 Arden Way, Suite 360, Sacramento, CA 95825
1870 No. Main Street, Suite 150, Salinas, CA 93906
464 West 4th Street, Room 348, San Bernardino, CA 92401
8765 Aero Drive, Suite 120, San Diego, CA 92123
30 Van Ness Avenue, Suite 3400, San Francisco, CA 94102
100 Paseo de San Antonio, Room 120, San Jose, CA 95113
28 Civic Center Plaza, Room 625, Santa Ana, CA 92701
411 E. Canon Perdido, Room 3, Santa Barbara, CA 93101
50 "D" Street, Suite 360, Santa Rosa, CA 95404
31 E. Channel Street, Room 317, Stockton, CA 95202
6150 Van Nuys Blvd, Room 100, Van Nuys, CA 91401

The Commercial Audition

Okay, it's finally here. The moment you've been training for. You practiced those commercials. You have an agent. You have great pictures with a résumé stapled on the back. You have a work permit. You're ready for a job! The phone rings. You rush to answer it.

You   - Hello?
Agent - Hey *(your name)*. I got a call from Dominos Pizza. They loved your picture and want to see you today at 3pm.
You   - Great!
Agent - Dress casual. You are playing a kid who goes with his family to Dominos only to find out that Dominos delivers. You got it, *(your name)*?
You   - Sure. When do I get the lines?
Agent - They'll be at the audition. (She gives you the address.) Good luck.

So you put on your best casual clothes and head to the audition. On the way there you do tongue twisters to get warmed up.

Step #1 - Get warmed up before you audition.

Then at 2:45 you arrive at the audition. (You'll need time to memorize your script.)

Step #2 - Always arrive 15 minutes early.

You look around. There are 15 other kids your age all standing around dressed in casual clothes. Oh no! The competition. A thought comes rushing into your head. What do I do now?

Sign in. There should be a sign-in sheet around. Make sure you sign in for the right commercial. Sometimes in Los Angeles there are as many as 10 commercials being cast in the same building. So make sure you sign up for Dominos.

Step #3 - Sign in.

The next thing you do is see if there are any scripts. Not all commercials have lines. But if they do, you want to start working on them as soon as possible.

Step #4 - See if there is a script.

You look around and find, right next to the sign-up sheet, a script for Dominos.

DOMINOS

I love babysitting my little brother. Because whenever I do, my mom pays me by buying me a pizza from Dominos. *(Looking at the crib)* Hey, buddy, look what I got. Your favorite pepperoni pizza. Oh, look at him smile. He is so cute. Coochy, coochy, coo. *(The baby grabs the piece of pizza)* Hey, that's my piece. Give it back! Okay, you can have it, but next time I'm ordering anchovies. He hates anchovies.

So you start memorizing. You want to be ready when the casting director calls you.

Step #5 - Start memorizing your script and thinking about how you are going to perform it.

After about five minutes, you have it down. Your training is really working. You know exactly what you are going to do when you go in the audition room.

The Commercial Audition

The casting director walks into the lobby and calls the names of a couple of kids sitting next to you. As they walk into the audition room they each lay down a piece of paper. You glance at it. What is it? It looks like a cartoon strip (see Storyboard Graphic on pages 70-71).

This is called a storyboard. It shows the actor exactly what the director is looking for. Look at each frame. See how the character of the kid changes in each frame. After you memorize the commercial, memorize the storyboard.

Step #6 - Look at the storyboard and memorize the action.

A couple of minutes later the casting director comes back into the lobby and calls your name. You walk into the audition room. The casting director asks you to stand on a piece of tape on the floor facing the camera. You do. You are nervous and excited.

Then the casting director says, "SLATE".

Note: To "slate" is to say your name and your agent's name.

Example slates.

"Hi. I'm Chuck Coplin and I'm with BBA."

"How's it goin'? I'm Lynn Larsen and I'm with the Judy Savage Agency."

"Mark Allen Stalbach. TGI Agency."

Always smile!

EXERCISE: - PRACTICE GIVING YOUR SLATE. GIVE IT YOUR OWN PERSONAL TOUCH. PRACTICE IT UNTIL YOU FEEL COMFORTABLE.

A good slate is very important. It is the first impression you make. You want to come across as professional and also fun to work with.

EXERCISE - DO YOUR SLATE IN FRONT OF A FRIEND.

Ask your friend what kind of impression you made. Did you get the response you wanted? If not, change your slate until you appear both professional and a fun person to hang around.

Things <u>not</u> to do while slating.

- Scratch
- Chew gum
- Frown
- Mumble

After you slate, the casting director will ask you to perform the Dominos commercial.

You nail it! All those months of training have paid off.

"Great" she says. "But can you look at the camera more and the baby less? And when the baby takes your pizza, don't get angry. Be more like 'Oh well' ".

———

The Commercial Audition

There is only one way to take direction from casting directors. Do *exactly* what they tell you to do. It is that simple. The director of the commercial has told the casting director exactly what she wants. It is the casting director's job to find an actor who can give the director what she is looking for.

EXERCISE - MEMORIZE THE DOMINO'S COMMERCIAL.

First practice performing it the way you think it should be. Then pretend that the casting director has given you one of the following *notes.*

- Laugh when the baby takes your pizza.
- Cry when the baby takes your pizza.
- Make funny faces when you say, "Coochy, coochy coo".
- Tease the baby with the pizza.
- Be embarrassed when the baby takes the pizza.
- Be mad when the baby takes the pizza.

Keep performing the commercial until you have tried all of the *notes.*

How did you do? If you had trouble, keep working on it. An actor must be able to perform in hundreds of different ways. When you walk into an audition, you are never 100% sure what the casting director wants. So be flexible. Try any note they give you.

EXERCISE - PICK ANY COMMERCIAL IN THIS BOOK. MEMORIZE IT. THEN MAKE A LIST OF 10 DIFFERENT WAYS YOU COULD PERFORM IT.

For example, happy, silly, sad or angry.

After you have made your list, perform the commercial all ten ways.

———

Okay, back to the audition. You take the casting director's notes and do exactly what she said.

"Great." she says, "Thank you. Callbacks are tomorrow."

You leave the audition room happy. You survived your first audition. You not only survived it, you excelled. Aren't you glad I made you memorize all those commercials?

Now comes the worst part of being an actor: waiting for the phone to ring.

The casting director said the "callbacks will be tomorrow." A callback is another audition, but this time for the director. It is the last step before you get the job. Hopefully you will get a callback. But if you don't, don't worry about it. There is always another audition. And as anyone who has ever watched television knows, there is always another commercial.

Example: Commercial Storyboard

'I love babysitting my little brother. Because whenever I do,
my mom pays me by buying me pizza from Dominos."

"He is so cute. Coochy, Coochy coo.
Hey that's my piece."

Example: Commercial Storyboard

"(Looking at the crib) Hey buddy, look what I got. Your favorite pepperoni pizza. Ohhh. . . look at him smile!"

"Hey give it back. Okay, you can have it but next time I'm ordering *anchovies*. He *hates* anchovies."

The Inside Scoop

Interviews with Two Hollywood Insiders

The Inside Scoop

Here is an interview with Debbie Palmer, the head of the Commercial Department at TG/Youth which is one of the best agencies in Los Angeles. Read my interview with her and hear from an agent what she's looking for in kid actors. (My questions are in italics, her answers follow.)

WHAT SCHOOL DID YOU GO TO? University of Southern Mississippi

WHAT WAS YOUR MAJOR? Journalism

WHEN DID YOU MOVE UP TO LA? January of 1991

WHEN DID YOU START WORKING IN THIS BUSINESS? I started with the Twentieth Century Artists Agency. I was an assistant to the agents for 3-1/2 years working in the children's division.

WHAT DID YOU LEARN AS AN ASSISTANT? When I came to LA, I had no agency background or experience. In order to get a job at a talent agency, generally they want people with experience. It's very rare that you can go into an agency without experience. This work is very demanding and they want someone that they can train on their own. They would not have you come from a place where they have other ways of doing something. I had a unique opportunity to get started in this business. I was lucky. I learned many many things there but I would have to say that a lot of stuff that has made me a better agent was learned after the fact. I didn't have opportunities to learn about re-negotiations and those kind of things until later.

NOW YOU'RE AN AGENT WITH TGI? Yes, Talent Group Incorporated or TGI Youth Division. I'm head of the Commercial Department.

HOW MANY CLIENTS DO YOU HAVE? I represent approximately 300 clients ranging from infancy to early 20's.

DO YOU HAVE ANY FAMOUS KIDS IN YOUR DEPARTMENT? Absolutely! I'm very proud of the caliber of talent we've been able to represent. In our commercial department we have Ashley Peldon from *The*

The Inside Scoop

Pretender, Miko Hughes of the films _Apollo 13, Mercury Rising_ and _Pet Semetary,_ Courtney Peldon and Taran Smith from _Home Improvement,_ Patrick Renna of _The X Files,_ Billy Sullivan and Michael Sullivan from _Seventh Heaven,_ Blake Ewing of _Ragtime_ and _The Little Rascals,_ Shawna Waldron of _Little Giants_ and _The American President,_ Dana Daurey of _Happily Ever After._ Then let's see there is—Ariana Richards of _Jurassic Park,_ Hilary Duff of _Casper Meets Wendy_ (Hilary plays Wendy), Marcus Paulk on _Moesha,_ Scarlett Polmers on _Star Trek Voyager,_ Shane Sweet on Nickelodeon's _Journey of Allen Strange,_ Josh Evans on _Ally McBeal_ and Aria Curzon and Stephanie Sawyer from _The Prince of Egypt._

WOW! HOW DID YOU FIND THESE KIDS? A lot come through client referrals. And I also go through every piece of mail I get. As well as attend showcases as often as I can.

WHAT KIND OF KIDS DO YOU LOOK FOR? We represent kids of all types: cute, quirky, fat, pretty. It varies. You have different age categories, different looks. We want REAL Kids. We don't look for "picture perfect" kids with every hair in place. Big ears are good!

WHAT HAPPENS AFTER YOU SEE THEIR PICTURE AND YOU LIKE THEM? An interview would be set up for him/her. They would interview with all four of our agents. Our agency is full service. We represent kids for commercials, voice-overs, television and film roles.

WHAT DO THEY DO WHEN THEY WALK IN THE DOOR FOR AN INTERVIEW? If they are 3 or 4 years old, we see how well they follow directions. We'll ask them to recite things like "Simon Says" or repeat "I love McDonald's". The kids 4 and older, they come in and we give them a commercial to work on, like one of the commercials that you have in your book. They will practice it and will come in by themselves. They don't have to have it memorized, they can hold the paper in their hands. If they're 6, then they have to have it memorized. After they do it once we may give them more direction. You know tell them different ways we want them to read it.

WHAT DO YOU JUDGE THEM ON? Several things: how well they follow directions. So, if they're on a set—if you can imagine that we're on the set and I'm the director—okay I say, "Take two steps and stand here", because that is what life is going to be like as an actor on a set.

HOW IMPORTANT ARE CLASSES TO KIDS? Classes are very important. An actor can never take enough classes. No matter if you're on a series. We have clients that are in series and feature films that continually practice their craft. You can never study enough.

EVEN KIDS? Absolutely!

HOW MUCH DO KIDS MAKE WHEN THEY DO COMMERCIALS? That's like a typical question that a parent would ask. There's no way to say that you'll make "X" amount of dollars on this job. Let's put it this way: a few nationals, depending on how long they have been on, can pay for college or buy a home for the future. Commercials usually run for 21 months. There's so many factors to that question that it's hard to pinpoint. I can't tell you that it's $26,750.00, but I can tell you that it can be a lot of money.

The Inside Scoop

Here is an interview with Jeff Gerrard, president of the Commercial Casting Directors Association. He has cast over 2500 commercials, many of them with kids. He has also cast films, television and stage. Mr. Gerrard is based in Los Angeles. (My questions are in italics, his answers follow.)

FIRST THING'S FIRST. GIVE US SOME BRAND NAMES OF COMMERCIALS YOU HAVE CAST. Playstation, Pepsi, World Class Wrestling, Yahoo.com, Nintendo, Life Cereal, Kelloggs, Sizzler, McDonalds. Truly, if you mention a product, we've probably cast it.

IN MY BOOK, 24-CARAT COMMERCIALS, EVERYTHING YOUR KIDS NEED TO KNOW TO BREAK INTO COMMERCIALS, WE TALK ABOUT THE IMPORTANCE OF GREAT HEAD SHOTS. WHAT DO YOU LOOK FOR IN A HEADSHOT? Naturalness. Nothing big or over the top. Never holding any props like soda cans or anything like that. Obviously, if the kid is a world class skateboarder then he should do a little insert in the bottom of the picture showing him doing a trick on a skateboard. Something that would really get him noticed. But being natural is most important.

WHEN A KID HAS AN AUDITION, WHAT SHOULD THEY EXPECT? The important thing to remember is to be professional. Here is the basic format: You get a call from your agent or manager. They say, "Go to Jeff Gerrard Casting at Big House Studios." Then when they show up there is a big lobby and a bulletin board with 2 to 5 jobs on it. It might say, "Coke, Nintendo, McDonalds". You have to then find the job your agent told you about. Sometimes actors show up and forget to ask their agent what commercial they are auditioning for. So they show up and there are 5 commercials. Well, then they look like a fool. But let's say you are auditioning for Nintendo. You walk over and first see if there are any lines for the Nintendo commercial. Don't sign in first! Many actors, adults as well as kids make this mistake. First find the lines. Then go over them. Be ready. Then and only then, when you really know the commercial, sign in. It's a good idea to show up 15 minutes early so you can learn your lines and still be on time. Also, make sure you fill out a size card. (That's a card that lists all of the actor's sizes: shoe, pants, etc.) And have your picture and résumé ready. I'll need that when you walk through the door. But really, before you sign in, make sure that you are ready. That you know your dialogue. This is the biggest mistake actors make. The other mistake is being late. When I cast a commercial, I have set times for each category. Let's say you have a four o'clock appointment but you show up at six. Well by six I might be working with infants. I'm not going to stop and see you. Be on time.

OKAY, SO NOW THEY ARE READY, THEY'VE SIGNED IN. WHAT HAPPENS WHEN THEY WALK IN THE DOOR TO SEE YOU? When they walk in, they will either meet me or an associate. And we will explain the commercial to them. We'll run the copy a couple of times to warm them up. The only times we don't warm them up is when they have to improv a scene or for a commercial where they have to eat something. In those cases, I like to go ahead and turn the camera on. But in most cases we warm the actors up. It's like theatre. The more times you rehearse, the better. Actors are always better on take 3 than on take 1.

OKAY SO THE YOUNG ACTOR AUDITIONED FOR YOU. THEY DID A GREAT JOB. THE NEXT DAY THE AGENT CALLS AND SAYS THEY HAVE A CALLBACK. WHAT HAPPENS THEN? Wear the same outfit you wore to the first call. You don't know why you got the callback. Was it your acting? Was it your look? Your hair? So don't get your hair shaved if you know the next day you might have a callback. Try to stick to what you did the first time because that is why they brought you back. With kids we are always looking at their own unique personality. Hopefully they will pick you.

This may be the end of the book, but for you it is just a beginning. I remember when I booked my first commercial. I was so excited about the chance to be on television. Throughout the 50 commercials and 100 plays I've performed in, that excitement has never left me. And I'm willing to bet, if you did all the exercises in this book, it will never leave you either.

Commercials are fun but they aren't the only way to be an actor. I want to encourage you to get involved with your local theaters. School plays and community theater are where most actors learn to act. There are very few things in life more fun than being on stage, in a great play, performing for hundreds of people. If you need any help with an audition monologue, I have written another book called MAGNIFICENT MONOLOGUES FOR KIDS, (see page 90), that will really help you.

Good luck.

Hey, wait a minute! Now that you're an actor, I should say what every actor hears on opening night.

Break-a-leg!

Glossary of Industry Terms

Show business has its own interesting vocabulary. The word *wings*, for example. When someone tells you to go *stand in the wings*, they mean stand on the *side of the stage,* not on the wings of a bird. I asked a number of the kids I coach to tell me their definitions for some of these important theater/film words. Sometimes kids can explain things more clearly than adults.

AD LIB - To make up words not already in the script. If a director tells you to ad lib, what he means is ignore the script and say something your character would say.

AFTRA - Stands for the "American Federation of Television and Radio Artists". AFTRA is a union for actors.

AGENT - A person who helps you get acting jobs. And then takes 10% of your earnings.

AIR DATE - The date that your commercial shows on TV.

ATMOSPHERE - See "Extra".

AUDITION - The show biz word for "trying out" for a commercial.

BEAt - A moment. If the script says: "A beat," then that means take a small pause before you say your next line.

BLOCKING - Stage Movement. When the director gives you blocking he is telling you where to stand and when to move.

BOOK - When you "book" a commercial that means that you have "won" the audition.

BOOM - A microphone that is held above your head.

BREAK-A-LEG - An actor's way of saying "Good Luck".

Glossary of Industry Terms

CALLBACK - The second audition.

CASTING DIRECTOR - The person hired by the producer to find the right actors for the job.

CATTLE CALL - See "Open Call".

CLIENT - The person who has final say on a commercial. If it is a Pepsi commercial then Pepsi is the client.

CUE - Any signal that it is your turn to speak or move. If the director says "pick up your cues", he means that when the other actor stops talking, you must start quicker.

CUE CARD - A piece of poster board with the actor's lines on it.

DIALOGUE - The lines you speak from your script.

DIRECTOR - The person who is in charge of the play or film. He or she instructs the actors, set designers and every other part of the play or film.

EXTRA - A nonspeaking part. An extra appears in the background of the scene. Also called Atmosphere.

FOCUS - Putting all your attention on one thing. If a director yells "focus", he/she mean "Listen up".

GESTURE - The way you move your arms and hands.

HAND PROPS - Small things used by the actor. Like a purse or a baseball.

HEADSHOT - An 8" X 10" black and white picture of an actor.

IMPROVISATION - Acting without a script. Making it up as you go along.

LINES - The words you speak from the script. Learning your lines means to memorize the speeches your character has in the script.

Glossary of Industry Term

OPEN CALL - An audition where you don't need an appointment. Also called a *Cattle-call* because open calls usually have tons of people.

PRINCIPAL - The main acting role in a commercial.

RESIDUAl - Money paid to an actor for the repeat showing of a commercial or TV show.

SAG - Stands for "Screen Actors Guild." SAG is a union for actors.

SIDES - Part of a script. When you audition, they give you sides to read from.

SLATE - What the casting director says at the beginning of a commercial audition. It means say your name and what agency represents you.

STAND-IN - Extras who "stand in" for the lead actors while the crew focuses lights.

TOP - The beginning. When the director says, "Go from the top", he means start at the beginning.

UPGRADE - Being "upgraded" means when you are hired as an extra and the director gives you a line or makes you a principal.

California
(Northern California)

Marla Dell Talent Agency
2124 Union St.,
Ste C
San Francisco, CA 94123
415-563-9213

Mitchell Agency
323 geary St
Ste 302
San Francisco, CA 94102
415-395-9475

Look Talent
166 geary St.
San Francisco, CA 94108
415-781-2841

San Francisco Top Models and Talent
870 Market street
Ste 1076
San Francisco, CA 94102
415-391-1800

Stars Agency
777 Davis Street
San Francisco, CA 94111
415-421-6272

South of Santa Fe Talent Guild
6921-B Montgomery NE
Albuqerque, NM 87109
505-880-8550

Tonry Talent
885 Bryant St.
Ste. 201
San francisco, CA 94103
415-543-3797

(Los Angeles)

Acme Talent
6310 San Vicente Blvd
Ste 520
LA, CA 90048
213-954-2263

Angel City Talent
1680 N. Vine St
Ste. 716
Hollywood, Ca 90028
213-463-1680

Bloom at Ford
8826 burton Way
Beverly Hills, CA 90211
310-859-9300

Bobby Ball Agency
4342 Lankershim Blvd
Universal City, CA 91602

Coast to Coast Talent Group
3350 Barham Blvd
Los Angeles, CA 90068
213-845-9200

Commercials Unlimited Inc
9601 Wilshire Blvd
Ste 620
Beverly Hills, CA 90210
310-888-8788

Coleen Cler Agency
178 S. Victory Blvd
Suite 108
Burbank, CA 91502
818-841-7943

CNA and Associates
1925 Century Park E.
Ste. 750
Los Angeles, CA 90067
310-556-4343

Cunningham-Escott-Dipene and Assoc.
10635 Santa Monica
Ste -130, 135, and 140
Los Angeles, CA 90025

Epstein-Wyckoff -Corsa and Ross
280 S. Beverly Dr.
Ste 400
Beverly Hills, CA 90212
310-278-7222

Gold/Marshak/Liedtke Agency
3500 W. Olive Ave, #1400
Burbank, CA 91505
818-972-4300

Hollander Talent Group
3518 cahuenga Blvd, W #316
Los Angeles, Ca 90069
213-845-4160

Kazarian/Spencer and Associates
11365 Ventura Blvd,
Suite 100, Box 7403
Studio City, CA 91604

LA Talent
8335 Sunset Blvd
2nd Floor
LA, CA 90069
213-656-3722

Cindy Osbrink
4605 Lankershim Blvd
Ste 408
N. Hollywood, CA 91602
8-760-2488

Herb Tannen
8370 Wilshire Blvd, Ste 209
Beverly Hills, CA 90211
213-782-0515

Tyler Kjar Agency
10643 riverside Dr.
Toluca Lake, CA 91602
8-760-0321

Beverly Hecht Agency
12001 Ventura Place, #320
Studio City, CA 91604
8-505-1192

Privilege Talent Agency
9229 Sunset Blvd
Ste 414
W. Hollywood, CA 90069
310-858-5277

The Savage Agency
6212 Banner Ave
La, CA 90038
213-461-8316

TGI-Youth
6300 Wilshire Blvd.
Ste 1499
LA, CA 90048
213-852-9555

(South of LA)

Artists Managment Agency
1800 E. Garry, Suite 101
Santa Ana, Ca 92705
714-261-7557

Agency 2 Model and Talent
1717 Kettner Blvd
Ste 200
San Diego, CA 92110
619-291-9556

Berzon Talent Agency
336 E. 17th St.
Costa Mesa, CA 92627
714-631-5936

Burkett Agency
27001 La Paz Road, Ste 418
Mission Viejo, CA 92691
714-830-6300

Morgan Agency
129 W. Wilson street
Ste 202
costa Mesa, CA 92627
714-574-1100

Shamon Freitas And Company
9606 tierra Grande,
Ste 204
San Diego, Ca 92126
619-549-3955

Commercial Agents

San Diego Model Management Talent
Agency
438 Camino Del Rio S. #116
San Diego, CA 92108
619-296-1018

Northwest

E. Thomas Bliss and Assoc.
219 1st Ave So.
Ste 420
Seattle, WA 98104
206-340-1875

Southwest

Baskow Agency
2948 E. Russel Rd
Las Vegas, NV 89120
702-733-7818

Donna Baldwin Talent
2150 W. 29th Ave
Suite 200
Denver, CO 80211

Leighton Agency
2231 E. camelback Rd
Ste319
Phoenix, AZ 85016
602-224-9255

Lenz Agency
1591 E. Desert Inn Rd.
Las vegas, NV 89109
702-733-6888

The Mannequin Agency
2021 San Mateo Blvd, NE
Albuquerque, NM 87110
505-266-6823

Donna Wauhob Agency
3135 Industrial Road,
#234
Las Vegas, NV 89109
702-733-1017

Eastman Agency
560 W. 200 South
Salt Lake City, UT 84101
801-364-8434

Mid West

Talent Unlimited
4049 Pennsylvania
Ste 300
Kansas City, MO 64111

Talent Shop
30100 Telegraph Road
Ste 116
Bingham Farms, MI 48025
248-644-4877

Talent Plus
55 Maryland Plaza
St. Louis Mo, 63108-1501
310-367-5588

(Chicago Area)

Cunningham-Escott-Dipene and Assoc.
One East Superior St.
Ste 505
Chicago, IL 60611
312-944-5600

Ambassador Talent Agents
333 N. Michigan Ave.
Ste 303
Chicago, IL 60601
312-641-3491

Arlene Wilson Models
430 W. Erie
Ste 210
Chicago, IL 60610
312-573-0200

Harrisse Davidson and Associates
65 E. Wacker Place
Ste 2401
Chicago, IL 60601
312-782-4480

Lily's Talent Agency Inc
5962 N. Elston
Chicago, IL 60646

Emila Lorence LTD
325 W. Huron,
Ste 404
Chicago, IL 60610
312-787-2033

North Shore Talent
454 Peterson Rd
Libertyville, IL, 90048
847-816-1811

Steward Talent Management
58 West huron
Chicago, IL 60610
312-943-0892

Salazar and Navas Inc - (Specializes in
Latino Children)
760 N. Ogden Ave,
Ste 2200
Chicago, IL 60622

(New England)

Classic Model and Talent Mgmt Inc
87 S. Finley ave
Basking Ridge, NJ 07920
908-766-6663

Model Club
115 Newbury Street, #203
Boston, Ma 02116
617-247-9020

Northeast
(New York)

Abrams Artists
420 Madison Ave
Ste 1400
New York, NY 10017
212-935-8980

Carson -Adler Agency Inc
250 W. 57th St.
Ste 808
New York, NY 10107
212-307-1882

Cunningham-Escott-Dipene and Assoc.
257 Park Ave South
Ste 900
New York, NY 10010
212-477-1666

J. Michael Bloom and Associates
233 Park Ave, So
10th FL.
New York, NY 10003
212-529-6500

Epstein-Wyckoff -Corsa and Ross
311 W. 43rd St.
Ste 304
New York, NY 10036
212-586-9110

Gilla Roos LTD
16 W. 22 Street
New York, NY 10010
212-727-7820

Rachael's Talent Agency INC
134 W. 29th St
Ste 903
New York, NY 10001
212-967-0665

Jordan, Gill and Dornbaum
156 Fifth Ave
Ste 711
New york, NY 10010
212-463-8455

McDonald Richards Inc
156 Fifth Ave
Ste 222
new York, NY 10010
212-627-3100

Fifi Oscard Agency
24 W. 40th St.
17th Fl
New York, NY 10018
212-764-1100

Sciffman, Ekman, MOrrison and Marx
22 W. 19 st. 8th Floor
New York, NY 10011
212-627-5500

South

Actors and Others Talent Agency
6676 Memphis-Arlington Rd.
Barlett, TN 38135
901-385-7885

Michele Pommier Models
927 Lincoln Road, #200
Miami Beach, FL 33139
305-672-9344

Acclaim Partners Inc
4107 Medical Parkway
Ste 210
Austin, TX 78756
512-323-5566

Actors Etc. Inc.
2620 Fountainview
Ste 210
Houston, TX 77057
713-785-4495

Atlanta Models and Talent
2970 Peachtree Rd NW,
Ste. 660
Atlanta, GA 30305
404-261-9627

Alexa Model and Talent Management
Inc
4100 W. Kennedy Blvd
Ste 228
Tampa, Fl 33609
813-289-8020

Azuree Talent Inc
140 N. Orlando Ave, #120
Winter Park, FL 32789
407-629-5025

Sandi Bell
2582 S. Marguire Rd.
Ste 171
Ocoee, FL 34761
407-656-0053

Boca Talent and Model Agency
829 SE 9th St.
DeerField Beach, Fl 33441
954-428-4677

Brevard Talent Group
405 Palm Springs Blvd
Indian Harbour Beach
FL 32937
407-773-1355

The Campbell Agency
3906 Lemmon Ave
Ste 200
Dallas, TX 75219-3760
214-522-8991

Kim Dawson Talent
2710 N. Stemmons Freeway, #700
Dallas, TX 75207-2208
214-630-5161

Dimensions 3 Modeling
5205 S. Orange Ave
Ste 209
Orlando, Fl 32809
407-851-2575

Dott Burns Talent Agency
478 Severn Ave
Tampa, Fl 33606
813-251-5882

Florida Stars Model and Talent
225 West University ave
Ste A.
Gainesville, FL 32601
352-338-1086

Fox-Evans agency
2010 Corporate Ridge
Ste 175
McLean, VA 22102
703-827-8071

Susanne Haley Talent
618 Wymore Rd, #2
Winter Park, Fl 32789
407-644-0600

Neal Hamil Agency
7887 San Felipe
Ste 227
Houston, Tx 77063
713-789-1335

Hurt Garver Talent
400 N. Newy York Ave
Ste 207
Winter Park, Fl 32789
407-740-5700

Glyn Kennedy inc
9700 Hunter Hills Dr
Roswell, Ga 30075
678-461-4444

Marquee Talent Inc
5911 Maple ave
Dallas. Tx 75235
214-357-0355

Martin and Donalds Talent Agency
2131Hollywood Blvd
Ste 306
Hollywood, FL 33020
954-921-2427

Quaid talent Agency
5959 richmond
Ste 310
Houston, TX 77057
213-936-8400

The People Store
2004 rockledge Road, NE
Atlanta, GA 30324
404-874-6448

Marian Polan Talent Agency
10 NE 11 Avenue
Ft. Lauderdale, FL 33301
954-525-8351

Stellar Model and Talent Agency
407 Lincoln Rd
STe 2K
Miami Beach , FL 33139
305-672-2217

Sherry Young/Mad Hatter Model and
Talent
2620 Fountainview
Ste 212
Houston, TX 77057
713-266-5800

Talent and Model Land
4516 Granny White Pike
Nashville, TN 37204
615-321-5596

Talent Trek
406 11th St
Knoxville, TN 37916
423-977-8735

Bibliography: Magnificent Performances By Young Actors

In my last book I listed my twenty-five favorite performances by young actors. Well, since then I've received letters suggesting many other great performances. So I've been watching a lot of films lately and added a few more to my list.

Will Wheaton, River Phoenix, Corey Feldman, Jerry O'Connell - <u>Stand by Me</u> (1986): Based on Steven King's "The Body". These four young actors do a great job bringing the 1950's to life. (R)

Jack Wild - <u>Oliver</u> (1968): Wild as 'The Artful Dodger" will make you want to run out and become a pick pocket. (G)

Tommy Kirk - <u>Old Yeller</u> (1957): When I saw this as a kid, I cried for hours afterwards. Tommy Kirk gives a heartbreaking performance as a boy who loves his dog.

Jurnee Smollett - <u>Eve's Bayou</u> (1997): Sassy and smart Jurnee Smollett is a vodoo priestess in training. A magical performance. (R)

Henry Thomas - <u>E.T. The Extra -Terrestrial</u> (1982): Watching Henry Thomas trying to hide E.T. is pure comic delight. (Watch for a young Drew Barrymore). (PG)

Ronny Howard - <u>The Music Man</u> (1962): This young actor, who is also great on *The Andy Griffith Show* is hysterical as Winthrup. Check out his song, "Gary Indiana". (G)

Christina Ricci -<u>The Addams Family</u> (1991) & <u>Addams Family Values (1993)</u>: Her deadpan interpretation of "Wednesday" is both chilling and funny. (Both Films PG-13)

Charlie Korsmo - <u>Dick Tracy</u> (1990): Korsmo does a great job as "The Kid". He's seen it all. Tough and tender. (PG)

Thomas Godet - <u>Toto le Hero</u> (1991): This French actor gives a simple but affecting performance. It's so simple that it doesn't even appear he is acting. Bravo. (PG)

Bibliography: Magnificent Performances By Young Actors

Natalie Wood - <u>Miracle on 34th St</u>. (1947): I've seen this film over 50 times and I never tire of seeing the look in Natalie Wood's eyes when she discovers Kris Kringle is really Santa Claus. (No rating)

Elijah Wood and *Thora Birch* in <u>Paradise</u> - (1991): Young love was never so sweet. (PG-13)

Tatum O'Neal - <u>Paper Moon</u> (1973): It's easy to see why she won an Oscar for this one. Part little girl. Part conman. She steals every scene she's in. (PG)

Huckleberry Fox - <u>Terms of Endearment</u> (1983): With just a look he breaks your heart. (PG)

Macaulay Culkin - <u>Home Alone</u> (1991): There is a reason this is one of the most popular films of all time. And that reason is Macaulay. (PG)

Travis Tedford - <u>The Little Rascals</u> : The original Little Rascals were big "over" actors. Travis makes Spanky funny and believable.

Sean Nelson - <u>Fresh</u> (1994): Sean Nelson witnesses a playground murder. This film is hard to watch. Very violent. But Sean Nelson's performance is fantastic. (R)

Ricky Schroder- <u>The Champ</u> (1979): One of the best criers in the business. Boy can this kid shed tears. (PG)

Karen Dotrice and *Matthew Garber* - <u>Mary Poppins</u> (1964): The two wonderful actors do a great job as Jane and Michael Banks. My favorite scene is when they jump into the magical sidewalk. (G)

Hayley Mills - <u>The Parent Trap</u> (1961): The original is still the best. No one plays twins better than Hayley Mills. (No rating)

Tina Majorino - <u>When a Man Loves a Woman</u> (1994): Tina is an amazing actress. Definitely one of my favorite performances. (R)

Bibliography: Magnificent Performances By Young Actors

Zelda Harris in <u>Crooklyn</u> - (1994): Zelda plays the only girl in a family with four boys. A strong performance by a wonderful young actress. (PG-13)

Michael Conner Humphreys - <u>Forrest Gump</u> (1994): Run Forrest Run. And he does. This kid has what it takes to be a great character actor. (PG-13)

Anna Paquin - <u>Fly Away Home</u> (1996): She won an Oscar for her work in <u>The Piano</u>. But my favorite performance of hers is in this little known classic. (PG)

Mary Badham and *Philip Alford* - <u>To Kill a Mockingbird</u> (1962): They are so real it doesn't seem like acting. (No Rating)

Justin Henry - <u>Kramer vs Kramer</u> (1979): He holds his own with Dustin Hoffman and Meryl Streep. (PG)

Peter Billingsley - <u>A Christmas Story</u> (1983): One of the most rented movies of all time. Peter Billingsley is perfect as the kid who wants a Red Ryder BB gun for Christmas. (PG)

Peter Ostrum - <u>Willy Wonka and the Chocolate Factory</u> (1971): The best for kids ever made. Peter Ostrum is the perfect Charlie. (G)

Jodie Foster - <u>Freaky Friday</u> (1977): Jodie switches personalities with her mother. (G)

Mara Wilson - <u>Mrs. Doubtfire</u>. (1993): All the kids are good in this hilarious film. But Mara Wilson has star power. (PG-13)

Whittni Wright - <u>I'll do anything</u>. (1994): She's both adorable and bratty. Not an easy combination to pull off. (PG-13)

Quinn Cummings - <u>The Goodbye Girl</u>. (1977): She's hysterical in this Neil Simon comedy. (PG)

Patty Duke - <u>The Miracle Worker</u>. (1962): She won an Oscar for her amazing portrayal of Helen Keller, a role she also played on Broadway. (No rating)

The full cast - <u>Bad News Bears.</u> (1976): What can you say about this lovable bunch of misfits? Except when I was kid they were my heroes. (PG)

24-Carat Commercials for Kids!
Everything Kids Need to Know To Break Into Commercials

&

Magnificent Monologues for Kids!
Everything Kids Need to Know To Get The Part

Postal Orders: Sandcastle Publishing & Distribution, Order Dept., P.O. Box 3070, South Pasadena, CA 91030-6070

Ph./FAX MasterCard/VISA/Am.Express Orders: 800 891-4204
Please fill out form below and have your credit card # & expiration date handy.

Internet: WWW.sandcastle-online.com

Trade Distribution: Sandcastle Distribution 323-255-3616
Competitive discount schedule, terms & conditions. Will work from purchase orders then invoice. STOP orders okay. USPS, UPS, Express service available.

Please send the following books.

Number of books ordered: _____ Cost of Books: $14.95 x _____ = _____
Sales Tax: (For California residents only)   = _____
  Please add 8.25% sales tax for books shipped to a California
  address. (That's $1.23 for one book, $2.46 for two, etc.)
Packaging/Shipping: $3.20 for first two books, $1.10/add'l book   = _____
                                                          Total   = _____

Check included: ☐
Please bill my credit card: ☐ MasterCard   ☐ Visa

Credit Card #: _ _ _ _ _ _ _ _ _ _ _ _ _ _ _ _

Expiration date: __ __/__ __
                 Month   Year

_____
Cardholder signature. (We must have your signature to process order.)

Customer Billing Information   ### *Ship To Information

Name: _____   Name: _____

Address: _____   Address: _____

City: _____   City: _____

State & Zip Code:_____   State & Zip Code: _____

Daytime Phone: (____) _____   * Please fill in the above if book(s) is to
                                        be shipped to someone/somewhere other
                                        than customer.